AFFIRMING

Paul Avis

ANGLICAN ORDERS AND THE PRIESTING OF WOMEN

Series Editor: Jeffrey John

DARTON · LONGMAN + TODD

First published in 1999 by
Darton, Longman and Todd Ltd
1 Spencer Court
140–142 Wandsworth High Street
London SW18 4JJ

in association with

Affirming Catholicism
St Luke's Centre
90 Central Street
London EC1V 8AQ

© 1999 Paul Avis

ISBN 0-232-52309-6

The views expressed in this book are those of the author and do not necessarily reflect any policy of Affirming Catholicism.

Designed and produced by Sandie Boccacci
in QuarkXPress on an Apple PowerMac
Set in 10/12^{1}/2pt Times
Printed and bound in Great Britain by Page Brothers, Norwich

Affirming Catholicism

Affirming Catholicism is a movement (not an ecclesiastical party) which exists to do two things. We affirm our confidence in our Anglican heritage; and we seek to renew and promote the Catholic tradition within it. Our aim is to explore, explain and share with others both inside and outside the Church a lively, intelligent and inclusive Catholic faith. In the words of our Trust Deed:

> It is the conviction of many that a respect for scholarship and free enquiry has been characteristic of the Church of England and of the Churches of the wider Anglican Communion from earliest times, and is fully consistent with the status of those Churches as part of the Holy Catholic Church. It is desired to establish a charitable educational foundation which will be true both to those characteristics and to the Catholic tradition within Anglicanism ... The object of the foundation shall be the advancement of education in the doctrines and the historical development of the Church of England and the Churches of the wider Anglican Communion, as held by those standing within the Catholic tradition.

Our Publications

These are offered as one means of presenting Anglican Catholic teaching and practice in as clear and accessible a form as possible. Some cover traditional doctrinal and liturgical themes: others attempt to present a well-argued Catholic viewpoint on issues of debate currently facing the Church. There is a list of our series of booklets on page v.

The present series of books is provided, where appropriate, with summaries to sections and suggested questions which we hope will facilitate personal study or discussion in groups. Other most recent titles in the series are:

Introducing Richard Hooker and The Laws of Ecclesiastical Polity Martyn Percy
Making a Rule of Life John Gaskell
The Practice of Abortion: A Critique Michael Banner

To order these publications individually or on subscription, or for further information about the aims and activities of Affirming Catholicism, write to:

> The Secretary
> Affirming Catholicism
> St Luke's Centre
> 90 Central Street
> London EC1V 8AQ
>
> Tel: 0171 253 1138
> Fax: 0171 253 1139

Books in the Affirming Catholicism series

Affirming Confession John Davies

By What Authority? – Authority, Ministry and the Catholic Church Mark D. Chapman

Catholic Evangelism Stephen Cottrell

Catholicism and Folk Religion Jeremy Morris

Christian Feminism – An Introduction Helen Stanton

Christ in Ten Thousand Places – A Catholic Perspective on Christian Encounter with Other Faiths Michael Ipgrave

History, Tradition and Change – Church History and the Development of Doctrine Peter Hinchliffe

Humanity and Healing – Ministering to the Sick in the Catholic Tradition Martin Dudley

Imagining Jesus – An Introduction to the Incarnation Lewis Ayres

Is The Anglican Church Catholic? – The Catholicity of Anglicanism Vincent Strudwick

Is There an Anglican Way? – Scripture, Church and Reason: New Approaches to an Old Triad Ross Thompson

Lay Presidency at the Eucharist Benedict Green

'Making Present' – The Practice of Catholic Life and Liturgy Christopher Irvine

Marriage, Divorce and the Church Anthony E. Harvey

The Ministry of Deliverance Dominic Walker OGS

'Permanent, Faithful, Stable' – Christian Same-Sex Partnerships Jeffrey John

Politics and the Faith Today – Catholic Social Vision for the 1990s Kenneth Leech

Trinity and Unity Jane Williams

What is Affirming Catholicism? Jeffrey John

Why Women Priests? – The Ordination of Women and the Apostolic Ministry Jonathan Sedgwick

About the Author

Paul Avis is General Secretary of the Council for Christian Unity of the Church of England, Sub-Dean of Exeter Cathedral and Director of the Centre for the Study of the Christian Church. His books include *Faith in the Fires of Criticism* (DLT). He has recently edited *Divine Revelation* (DLT).

Contents

Acknowledgements viii

Introduction 1
Making the Case 2
Ongoing Dialogue 3
The Main Objections 5
Summary 7

Objections to Women Priests 8
The Argument from Unchanging Tradition 8
*The Argument from Limitations of Authority
in a Divided Church: Only the Whole Church Has
the Authority to Act* 12
The Argument from Ecumenical Relations 18
The Argument from the 'Liberal Agenda' 19
Summary 24

Anglican Orders and the Priesting of Women 26
*Is a Church which Ordains Women a True
Church? The Question of Apostolicity* 33
*How Secure Are the Orders of Women Priests? The
Question of Catholicity* 40
Summary 49

Questions 50

Bibliography 52

Acknowledgements

I would like to thank the Revd Canon Bill Croft, the Very Revd Richard Eyre, the Rt Revd Alec Graham, the Revd Professor Robert Hannaford and the Rt Revd Geoffrey Rowell for commenting on earlier drafts of this book. However, they should not be implicated in the views expressed here. A version of this chapter was read to a gathering of Affirming Catholicism in the Diocese of Bath and Wells at the Old Deanery, Wells, in May 1995. Material which has now found its way into the book was published in the *Church Times* in September 1996 for the centenary of *Apostolicae Curae*.

Introduction

For many people in the Church of England and the wider Anglican Communion at the turn of the twentieth century it is as natural as the sky is blue that women should be priests and should enjoy equality of ministry in the Church with men. Though a considerable number of Anglicans may have taken some time to adjust to this idea, seeing women deacons and priests going about their ministry of word, sacrament and pastoral care and taking part in the synodical government of the Church at deanery, diocesan and national level has defused the issue for them and now they cannot imagine what all the fuss was about. They cannot imagine a Church without women clergy. We might be forgiven for wondering, however, how many clergy and representative lay people (lay ministers and elected members of houses of laity in synodical bodies) would be able to give a reasoned theological defence of this major change in the way that the Church of England orders its ministry. We might suspect that the familiar but threadbare Anglican approach of benevolent pragmatism, rather than theological principle, is primarily responsible for the widespread acceptance of women's priestly ministry.

But benevolent pragmatism, if that is indeed the prevailing attitude, is not nearly enough to justify women priests. The majority who have no problem with women priests cannot help being aware that there is a substantial minority of Anglicans who are deeply upset about this development. They are naturally predisposed to regard them as Christians of sincerity and goodwill, but they may not be at all sure why these people should find the ordination of women misguided and damaging. They may be tempted, therefore, to dismiss this opposition as based on irrational prejudice, misogyny and blind conservatism and consider it unworthy of a considered response. I believe that we should resist that temptation. I am convinced that we should take reasoned objections to women's priesthood at their strongest and that we should continue to make out a convincing case, grounded in theological principles, for the ordination of women to the priesthood by the Church of England.

Making the Case
This approach seems to me to be all the more necessary because the Church of England by no means did all that it could to facilitate an informed and balanced discussion leading up to the decision. While the Church took plenty of time formally to consider the issues (about eighteen years on the narrowest interpretation) and conducted the debate through all the appropriate conciliar (synodical) channels at every level of the Church's conciliar life, from PCCs to General Synod, it made insufficient effort, in my view, to provide the theological and educational resources to enable its members to arrive at an informed, reflective and balanced decision. The House of Bishops published several reports, the last of these being a useful compendium of arguments for and against. But the Doctrine Commission was not put to work on any doctrinal implications; the Faith and Order Advisory Group was not

consulted about the ecumenical aspects; and the General Synod did not take the opportunity to set up a commission of all the talents that could have examined the theological, ecumenical and pastoral arguments for and against in a definitive way in the light of preparatory work done by these specialist bodies. When the legislation was finally put by the House of Bishops to General Synod in November 1992 it was not done in a manner calculated to allay the misgivings of conservatives. The least that was required was a substantial presentation marked by a sensitive awareness of the objections and a basic theological seriousness that none could gainsay. Regrettably, the presentation on behalf of the House did not do full justice to the requirements of substance, sensitivity and seriousness. The charge of theological levity, made by some opponents of the legislation, cannot be brushed aside, in my opinion.

Ongoing Dialogue

The lack of a full and rigorous examination of the theological issues, on the part of the Church of England officially, reinforces the need for a continued period of reception, discernment and dialogue, as provided for in the Episcopal Ministry Act of Synod 1993. I know that some Anglicans, especially women priests, are worried by the term 'reception'. They are dismayed at the implied suggestion that we cannot be sure whether it is right for the Church to ordain women to the priesthood. However, I believe myself that some degree of uncertainty is inevitable when we consider this step in the broader ecumenical perspective.

The fact that the two largest and most ancient communions that hold to the threefold order in historical succession, the Roman Catholic Church and the Eastern Orthodox Church, do not accept that women can be priests must give pause for thought. Objectively considered, this division in the mind of Christendom must concern all catholic-minded Anglicans. That does not mean that I am not personally fully convinced that the Church of England has done the right thing. It simply means that Churches should consider one another in their theologising and the actions that follow from that and be willing to learn from one another. The reception of the Reformation took four hundred years and at the end of that time many of Luther's most crucial reforms – though by no means all – were accepted in the Roman Catholic Church at Vatican II and through the ecumenical dialogues that followed.

Anglicans who know their tradition know that Anglican theology is not comfortable with the notion of certainty. Joseph Butler classically taught in the eighteenth century that 'probability is the guide of life' and that 'doubt is ever our portion in this life' (see further on probability, Avis, *Anglicanism and the Christian Church*, 1989, pp. 283–7). We cannot be objectively sure of most things in Christian belief – not even that the words attributed to Jesus in the Gospels were actually spoken by him or that the terms employed by the early ecumenical councils and embodied in the creeds to define his deity and humanity were the best ones. The truth cannot be discerned all at once in any area of faith. It takes time and tribulation and prayer and faithfulness and dialogue. I am convinced that through a process of discernment the truth that women are called to be priests will grow brighter and stronger. But that is obviously not how many thoughtful people see it. So during this period of reception, outstanding questions remain to be resolved, the continuing reservations and objections of the minority remain to be weighed and answered, and the anxieties of some remain to be allayed, if possible.

Some veteran campaigners for women's ordination believe that the time for dialogue with the opposition has passed and that to go on talking will achieve little. My own experience of engaging over a good many years with thoughtful opponents of women's ordination convinces me that continued dialogue is essential. It can clarify what is and what is not intended, correct misunderstandings, introduce individuals to arguments they may not have considered, and give reassurance, especially to laity and young clergy. A new generation of lay members of PCCs and synods, and of ordinands, requires and deserves to have the issues explored in a responsible way.

The Main Objections

There seem to be four main theological objections to the ordination of women by the Church of England:

(a) The argument from the authority of tradition: tradition on this fundamental matter of holy order confines the priesthood to males and this tradition cannot be changed.

(b) The argument from the limitations of authority in a divided Christian Church: only the whole Church has the authority to act in a fundamental matter; therefore in ordaining women, the Anglican Churches have exceeded their authority.

(c) The ecumenical damage argument: such unilateral action is damaging to ecumenical relations with those Churches that share with Anglicans an episcopal polity but oppose women's priesthood (the Roman Catholic and Eastern Orthodox Churches).

(d) The argument from the supposed liberal agenda of proponents of the ordination of women: women priests are the thin end of the feminist wedge which will undermine orthodox faith and order.

These are the arguments that carry weight with catholic-minded Anglicans. But there is also the argument from the patriarchal interpretation of 'headship', favoured by some conservative evangelicals, which connects with the presupposition found in traditional catholic theology (in St Thomas Aquinas, for example) that women are unfitted by nature to bear authority. For most reflecting Christians, that argument proves too much as it carries unacceptable consequences for the authority of women in the state and in society at large. It is not discussed further here since it really belongs within a milieu rather different from that of catholic Anglicanism (those interested in pursuing this aspect should look at Edwards, 1989, Hayter, 1987, and Avis, *Eros and the Sacred*, 1989).

I find each of these objections worthy of serious consideration. As a long-standing active supporter of women's priesthood, through the Movement for the Ordination of Women, through synodical action in my diocese and in the General Synod and through writing, I do not find them conclusive, but I believe they need to be fully addressed. I am not one of those who believe that the question of the ordination of women priests by the Church of England is 'an open and shut case', even though that does not lead me to have any doubts about the real priestly ministry of ordained women. So let us look at each of these objections in turn before we consider the implications, for our Church and its ministry, of the fact that the

Church of England, like some other provinces of the Anglican Communion, has – like it or not – ordained women priests.

> *Summary*
>
> The ordination of women by the Church of England requires theological justification. Though the Church conducted the process of consultation leading to the legislation through all the proper synodical or conciliar channels over a protracted period, it should have provided its members with more adequate theological resources to take a decision. A period of discernment, reception and dialogue, in which the ordination of women to the priesthood can be assessed in a broader ecumenical perspective, is now inevitable and this is reinforced by the Episcopal Ministry Act of Synod 1993. The objective uncertainty that this introduces into the situation is uncomfortable – especially for women priests – but squares with the traditional Anglican insistence that probability in matters of theological truth is our condition. Dialogue is as important as ever, for individuals cannot be expected to change their minds overnight and there is a new generation that requires to be convinced. This is the context in which the four main arguments against the ordination of women to the priesthood by the Church of England need to be considered.

Objections to Women Priests

(a) The Argument from Unchanging Tradition
There is a virtually unwavering tradition of the Church that women cannot be admitted to holy orders, for the priesthood is confined to males. I am not personally particularly impressed by fragments of evidence from the patristic or early medieval periods that may suggest the existence of some women clergy then. Even if substantiated, such cases would simply remain the exception that proved the rule.

For some who remain unconvinced about the ordination of women, this tradition of male-only clergy is so impressive in its antiquity and unanimity that it outweighs changes in the social position of women, considerations of rights and justice, and the question of women's complementary gifts. They regard all these as pragmatic arguments that cannot counter the decisive authority of tradition.

This is the official Roman Catholic position, expressed in the statement of the Sacred Congregation for the Doctrine of the Faith (CDF) *Inter Insigniores* in 1976. The Vatican acknowledged that it was dealing with an issue which classical theology had hardly touched upon, but nevertheless felt confident in claiming that 'the Catholic Church has never felt that priestly or episcopal ordination can be validly conferred on women' (Flannery, ed., 1982, pp. 332f.). The Sacred Congregation's verdict that 'the Church, in fidelity to the example of the Lord, does not consider herself authorized to admit women to priestly ordination' was based therefore not on explicit teaching in the past, but on the witness of the Church's practice which, it claimed, has a 'normative character'. There is, the CDF stated, an 'unbroken tradition throughout the history of the Church, universal in the East and in the West' (ibid., pp. 332, 338).

Other, subsidiary arguments are deployed in *Inter Insigniores* – particularly the claim that, just as there is a 'natural resemblance' between the element of bread and the body of Christ and the element of wine and the blood of Christ, so too there must be a 'natural resemblance' between Christ and the celebrant of the eucharist and that Christ's maleness as the man Jesus of Nazareth, even in his glorified state in heaven, rather than the humanity he assumed in the incarnation, is what counts as natural resemblance. But these tactics seem to have been played down in more recent statements. They are, of course, highly contestable and would not exclude women deacons. They give theological hostages to fortune.

The fundamental – and comparatively safe – argument of *Inter Insigniores*, based on unvarying tradition, has been reiterated in various recent papal statements where it is linked to the notion of the divine constitution of the Church – a blueprint laid down by Jesus Christ when he called twelve men and constituted them an apostolic college with Peter at their head – a well-worn theme of Roman Catholic ecclesiology, defined most recently in the decree *Lumen Gentium* of Vatican II. In a letter to all Roman Catholic bishops on 13 May 1994, the Pope stated: 'I declare that the Church has no authority whatsoever to confer priestly ordination on women and that this judgement is to be definitively held by all the Church's faithful.' As is well known, with these words the Pope formally put an end to all debate on this issue within the Roman obedience. The Pope's judgement is intended to be received with unquestioning loyalty as an irreformable (i.e. practically infallible) teaching of the Church.

We do not tend to find Anglicans coming out with these arguments from the authority of tradition. The argument from the apostolic constitution of the Church by Christ, as understood by Rome, proves too much for Anglicans as it entails buying the papacy with its claim to universal rule over the Church (universal ordinary and immediate jurisdiction), since the ministry of Peter is seen as the linchpin of the apostolic college. Indeed many Anglicans are open to the idea that there were socio-cultural reasons why Jesus chose only men as his apostles and they would not be convinced by the Vatican's argument in *Inter Insigniores* that non-theological factors should be excluded on the grounds that in other respects Jesus and Paul challenged social conventions.

Furthermore, many Anglicans, I suspect, would not be swayed in principle by an argument based solely on the authority of tradition. Tradition alone is not decisive in Anglican theological method. Anglicans would be wary of appearing to absolutise tradition. In Anglicanism, tradition is subject to Scripture and interpreted by reason. Without a central magisterium, beyond which there is no appeal, to decide what strands of the bewilderingly diverse Christian traditions are definitive and binding, tradition presents more questions than answers. As Hans Küng brought out in his discussion of papal infallibility, the Roman Catholic Church's ban on all artificial methods of birth control in

Humanae Vitae (1968) also rests on the authority of unanimous tradition (Küng, 1972) and Anglicans do not generally accept that conclusion. There is in fact a close parallel between the Vatican's arguments against women priests and those against artificial methods of birth control.

As the late Henry McAdoo, former Archbishop of Dublin and one of our greatest authorities on the Anglican theological tradition, points out, tradition is not only the Church remembering, but also the Church interpreting. In his discussion of the ordination of women in relation to tradition, McAdoo draws on the celebrated Anglican divines of the sixteenth, seventeenth and eighteenth centuries – John Jewel and Richard Hooker, William Laud and Henry Hammond, Richard Stillingfleet and William Wake, among others – to show that, for Anglicans, tradition has weight but not finality, that it guides our interpretation of Scripture but is itself subject to Scripture, that it is not self-authenticating but requires evaluation. Above all, McAdoo insists that tradition should not be absolutised. Conservative traditionalism is as dangerous as fundamentalist biblicism or arrogant rationalism. Both Scripture and tradition demand a hermeneutic, a method of interpretation. McAdoo argues that right interpretation is achieved through the 'authenticating interplay' that can be set up between the historical revelation given once for all supremely in Jesus Christ and reflected in Scripture, on the one hand, and the life of the Church in its mission carried out in diverse situations on the other. So change is inevitable but continuity is essential. There are, then, specific limits to the authority of tradition in Anglicanism which make any appeal to the authority of unanimous tradition *tout court* inappropriate.

In any case, Rome's insistence that unanimous tradition cannot be altered should be taken with a polite pinch of salt. The Roman Catholic Church does not really believe that major changes to tradition are impossible. After all, it was Rome that put the *Filioque* (the phrase 'and from the Son') in the Creed with disastrous ecumenical consequences – finally alienating the Eastern Churches who hold to the original form of that creed – and imposed the requirement of clerical celibacy. Perhaps that is another reason why the Roman line seems to have shifted slightly of late, from the authority of tradition as such to the narrower argument from tradition, the apostolic constitution of the Church by Jesus Christ.

Finally, Anglicans cannot make sense of the idea that any theological question could be foreclosed by Church authorities, in the way that Pope John Paul II has attempted to stifle discussion of the ordination of women. Anglicans cannot accept that any issue is 'off limits' for discussion. Anglicans prize their freedom of enquiry and debate in which radical and dissenting voices can gain a hearing. They will not want to silence the lone prophetic voice, for fear of quenching the Spirit.

(b) The Argument from Limitations of Authority in a Divided Church: Only the Whole Church Has the Authority to Act

This is probably the most common reservation expressed by catholic Anglicans who are not necessarily opposed to women priests under all circumstances. They argue that the threefold order in historical succession belongs to the heritage of the whole Church, therefore no single part of the Church has the authority to alter it. (This differs from the official Roman Catholic position that the Church simply has no authority to change the exclusive tradition of male priests.)

First let us freely admit that it would have been greatly preferable to have ordained women with the support of an ecumenical consensus. The claim that such a radical departure from universal tradition demands universal agreement has a certain initial plausibility. But the notion of ecumenical consensus – so attractive in theory – is profoundly problematic in practice. I would claim that the step taken by Anglican Churches in ordaining women has the degree of consent that can be reasonably expected. I invite consideration of the following points:

- The Roman Catholic Church has made it abundantly clear that it does not regard itself as 'authorized' to make this change to tradition. If Rome has insisted that there are no circumstances in which it could ever be right to ordain women priests (the Pope does not say deacons), the appeal to an ecumenical consensus is not just an argument for delay, but a somewhat disingenuous argument for delay *sine die*.
- Though in recent times there have been some women deacons in the Orthodox Churches, and this is now being encouraged in some parts of Orthodoxy, and, moreover, there are some Orthodox of the dispersion, such as Metropolitan Anthony Bloom, who are in favour of women priests, the Orthodox have generally been as hostile as Rome towards the Anglican decision to ordain women. Within Orthodoxy patriarchy prevails and there still linger oppressive traditions about the 'uncleanness' of menstruating women who may be present at the eucharist. Belief in the unchangeability of tradition is at

the very core of Orthodox ecclesial identity. It is difficult to foresee circumstances in which it would become possible for the Orthodox to welcome women priests. In relation to the Orthodox too, appeal to the emergence of ecumenical consensus smacks of special pleading.

- In a divided Christian Church there is at present no machinery in existence for the Churches to act together on fundamental questions of faith and order. Sometimes it is wistfully suggested that an ecumenical council could adjudicate on this issue, but that is just a dream. A council presupposes unity in faith and in oversight: it is an expression of communion. There can certainly be expressions of conciliarity – consultation and decision-making – between separated Churches, provided they recognise each other as Churches. Sadly, even that modest condition does not pertain between the Roman Catholic and Eastern Orthodox Churches on the one hand and the Anglican Communion of Churches on the other. While the Churches remain tragically divided they must perforce act 'unilaterally'. What that pejorative term means in practice is that each branch of the Church must act responsibly, in accordance with its conscience, and through its structures of conciliarity and decision-making in fulfilment of its mission. Churches have always acted unilaterally and they still do, rightly or wrongly. The Roman Catholic Church has acted unilaterally in recent times in all its dogmatic formulations, from papal infallibility and the Marian dogmas to *Humanae Vitae* and other recent pronouncements on sexual ethics. What is sauce for the goose is sauce for the gander.

There is a final irony in Anglicans condemning 'unilateral' action per se. In the sixteenth century, the English

Church acted on its sole authority in bringing in a thoroughgoing reform of belief, worship and Christian life within its borders. It did this in defiance of the popes who for centuries had frustrated reform. Reform was judged to be imperative if the consciences of Christian people were not to be further harmed. The position today over women priests is, I believe, closely analogous. It is the conscience of the Church (or at least of a substantial majority within the Church) that has compelled a similar unilateral action. I see the ordination of women as a reform of the ministry comparable to the reforms that were carried out in the sixteenth century. The Churches that were shaped by the Reformation insisted that a particular Church has the authority to reform itself without tarrying for Rome. That is the very *raison d'être* of Anglicanism. It is implied in the logic of the Reformation itself. At that time the structure of the ministry was modified in the light of a deeper understanding of what was and what was not required by the gospel, by Scripture and by primitive tradition. The jurisdiction of the pope was removed; clergy were permitted to marry; some minor orders were abolished.

Just as the sixteenth-century English Church acted in accord with the continental Lutheran and Reformed Churches, so the Church of England today has acted in accord with many sister Churches of the Anglican Communion. The precedent of the Reformation does not of course justify the particular decision regarding women priests – which has to be assessed on its merits – but it does, I think, establish the principle that unilateral action is sometimes justified. It certainly shows that no Anglican can condemn unilateral action *tout court* without condemning their own standing ground as an Anglican.

What scope do particular Churches have for making changes in their outward order? The Thirty-Nine Articles give to particular Churches authority in rites and ceremonies and in controversies of faith in matters that have been ordained by human authority (cf. Articles 20 and 34). McAdoo has argued that Richard Hooker, the prime architect of Anglican ecclesiology, recognised the authority of particular Churches to make changes in the received order of the Church, if the circumstances had changed (Hooker, 1845, vol. 3, p. 164: *Ecclesiastical Polity* VII.v.8), since for Hooker the universal Church subsisted only in particular Churches so that when a particular Church acts, that is the Church acting – the only way it can act. McAdoo's interpretation is not uncontested, and it seems to me that we cannot be quite certain of the correct interpretation of Hooker at this point. However, it seems highly probable that he believed with the mainstream Reformers, both continental and English, that particular or national Churches had the authority and the duty to reform themselves and order their affairs according to their lights and that this power included changes in the sphere of order, though not of doctrine (McAdoo, 1997).

It is often claimed that doctrine is actually at stake in the ordination of women – and that Anglicans have made a new doctrine by saying that women can be priests. I do not believe that the ordination of women is a doctrinal matter at all. Whatever some may say, there is no received doctrinal position, conveyed to us by tradition, that maleness is intrinsically necessary to the ordained priesthood. There is no credal or conciliar issue at stake here. Doctrinal change is not involved in the action of a Church that has decided to remove the bar to women being ordained. No Christian Church claims the authority to articulate new doctrines. The Church of England would not have proceeded in this matter if it had believed that it was innovating in doctrine. But the interpretation and application of doctrine to practice is going on all the time. The historic faith must be interpreted afresh in each generation. It is that process of interpretation and application that is involved here. It is not a question of faith but of order – and even then it is not a challenge to the received principles of holy order. Churches that have the threefold order of bishops, priests and deacons in historical succession do not believe that they have the right to tamper with that. Anglicanism is committed to the historic threefold ministry and certainly does not wish to undermine it. The ordination of women is not a fundamental change in the received ordering of the Christian ministry, but simply a reform of practice in the sphere of order. The historic threefold ministry is surely capacious enough to incorporate women who have passed through the same process of calling, testing, training and commissioning as men.

Even the Roman Catholic Church clearly believes that the Church can and should, when necessary, reform the structure of its ministry. The Second Vatican Council (1962-5) abolished some minor orders, just as the Reformers did. It also renewed and altered its teaching about the episcopate and its collegiate structure, making the bishop the paradigm of ordained ministry and its full embodiment and developing a theology of the diocese as the local church (see Osborne, 1988, ch. 11). Similarly, the Eastern Churches have become more open in recent years to the possibility of admitting (or possibly readmitting) women to the diaconate. There is nothing controversial about particular Churches or communions of Churches making changes in the structure of their ministry. Church order is not fossilised. Historical forms are not absolute. If only the Church of England had been able to explain what it was doing at the time in those terms!

(c) The Argument from Ecumenical Relations

What we might call 'the ecumenical damage argument' is a subdivision of a 'whole Church' approach. As we come to the end of this ecumenical century in which separated Churches have grown in mutual respect, understanding and affection, and have made considerable progress in overcoming doctrinal differences through ecumenical dialogue, is it responsible to jeopardise this achievement? Why put the roadblock of the ordination of women in the path of further convergence? Why create this gratuitous affront to Rome and the Orthodox? This is a pragmatic response, but certainly not to be despised for that.

This argument has weight since both Rome and the Orthodox have made it clear that the ordination of women by the Church of England has created a fresh obstacle to further convergence (the exchange of letters between the Archbishop of Canterbury and the Pope on this point is printed as an appendix to Eames, 1989). Without in any way discounting the strong convictions in play here, Anglicans might point out that this stance is not completely logical. Even allowing for the fact that actions taken by the Church of England may have a particular impact, it remains the case that dialogue with Rome (through the Anglican-Roman Catholic International Commission – ARCIC), and with the Orthodox (in the Anglican-Orthodox Joint Doctrinal Commission), is not conducted by the Church of England alone, but by the whole Anglican Communion which already had women priests and even women bishops before 1992.

The ecumenical damage argument also, in my view, is lacking in realism. It betrays the familiar Anglican sentimentality about the Roman and Eastern traditions. There is an inveterate tendency among a certain kind of Anglican to imagine fondly that the grass is greener on the other side of the ecumenical divide. The unpalatable truth is, however, that neither of these great communions even properly recognises the Church of England as a Christian Church, with authentic ministries and sacraments. They are not being prevented from embracing the Churches of the Anglican Communion as sister Churches by their ordination of women. Rome holds that Anglicanism lacks the fullness of the means of salvation. It is not about to recognise even the orders of Anglican male priests. While the Second Vatican Council acknowledged 'a real though imperfect communion' established with non-Roman Christians through baptism, the Orthodox have never committed themselves to any formal evaluation of the ecclesial status of the Anglican Churches. To put the issue in that way reinforces the need for the Church of England to uphold its position as a true and apostolic Church of Christ that, therefore, does indeed have authentic ministries and sacraments and, moreover, has sufficient authority within itself to make canonical provision to ordain whomsoever it responsibly judges to be fit subjects for ordination.

(d) The Argument from the 'Liberal Agenda'
Some Anglican objectors to women's priesthood claim to

see it as a capitulation to a radical liberal agenda, along with such supposedly liberal shibboleths as approval of homosexuality, theological relativism, political correctness, etc. Their suspicions are not entirely without foundation! As Mark Chaves has shown in *Ordaining Women: Culture and Conflict in Religious Organizations*, campaigns for the ordination of women have usually been a response to cultural and social pressures, one way of responding to post-Enlightenment liberalism, an ideological gesture.

The book actually challenges both proponents and opponents of the ordination of women and its findings should provide both constituencies with much food for thought. Research, combining Church history with organisational theory, into the roles allotted to women in one hundred American denominations – particularly biblicist and sacramentalist ones – during the past hundred years produces some highly paradoxical conclusions, that are of wider relevance. Generally they demonstrate that support for or opposition towards women's ministry is not governed chiefly by theological principles but tends to be ruled by non-theological factors, and in particular by an overall stance vis-à-vis modern progressive liberalism.

Chaves' research shows, for example, that the opening up of ministerial office to women is not generally directly related to a shortage of male clergy, and therefore to pastoral requirements, but if anything, quite the reverse. Similarly, the number of women studying theology and offering themselves for ordination is not related to whether or not their Church encourages this. Moreover, the extent to which women function ministerially is not a direct reflection of the place formally allowed them by a

Church: function and office are 'decoupled' (as we see, I suggest, in the case of women pastoral assistants in the Roman Catholic Church who are deacons in all but name). Chaves believes that the symbolic significance of women's ordination, as signalling an overall stance vis-à-vis liberal values, far exceeds the practical difference it makes in the life of a Church. He shows that the likelihood of a Church ordaining women can be predicted sociologically, being related to its degree of decentralisation: the distribution of power – its centralisation or dispersal – is a function of the strength of patriarchy, which liberalism is committed to overthrowing. Even when a decision to ordain women has been taken by a Church, that does not mean that all positions are automatically open to them: their ordination is a gesture towards liberalism, not a root and branch reform of Church structures.

The same piece of research suggests that conflicts about women's ordination are not about women as such – opposition to women priests should not be attributed to sheer misogyny – but about the question of gender differences and similarities. There is a small industry researching this, but there remains enormous personal, psychological and sociological investment in the views that people hold on gender identity. Conservatives tend to maximise gender dualism, stereotypes and clear boundaries, while liberals tend to favour gender complementarity or psychological androgyny (a technical term that refers not to bisexuality or physical hermaphroditism, but to the idea that personality characteristics belong to a common humanity rather than to one sex: see Avis, 1989), on the other. The issue of gender equality has served as a litmus test of a Church's attitude towards liberal modernity, how it defines itself in the modern world.

Only in the first wave of the women's movement at the beginning of the century, in the struggle for women's suffrage, Chaves points out, did gender equality become attached to the liberal agenda of individual human rights. The stance adopted by conservative Churches – Protestant biblicist or Catholic sacramental – towards women ministers functioned as a way of constructing organisational identity and cohesion over against liberal modernity. It signalled commitment to a particular supposedly static institutional world that was defined in opposition to modernity. This interpretation is borne out by the fact that militant opposition to gender equality in the realm of the sacred spans religions and cultures, being found in Islam and Judaism, for example, as well as in Christianity.

In legitimating this response to liberal ideology, both Protestant biblicist and Catholic sacramentalist Churches appealed to infallible divine authority. Protestants tended to appeal to the authority of Scripture interpreted without benefit of modern historico-critical methods, while Catholics invoked the authority of tradition interpreted by the magisterium (pope and bishops). Since the general principle of gender equality and human rights is universally acknowledged by western Churches (nowhere more so than by the Roman Catholic Church since Vatican II), divine authority has to be invoked in order to make an exception of women's ordination. Chaves adduces evidence both theological and sociological to show that this exception is illogical and incoherent. But that turns out to be not a victory for campaigners for women priests! Their agenda also is shown in this work to have been more a response to a liberal environment outside the Church, in order to demonstrate liberal credentials to a society concerned about human rights, than one grounded in either theology or pastoral needs.

Now that modernity is giving way to postmodernity – an intensification of the self-critical, reflexive, subversive dynamic of modernity – the argument needs to move on. As the progressive liberal agenda fades, a new challenge is taking its place. Postmodernism, the cultural vanguard of postmodernity, presents a major threat to all forms of Christian coherence. It is corrosive of the essential ecclesiological principles of tradition, doctrine, community and authority. Church people are notoriously prone to fighting the battles of yesterday. It is sad to see liberals uncritically echoing a modernist agenda: the ordination of women is not about individual human rights – for ordination cannot be a right for any individual or group – but about realising the fullness of Christ in all the baptised members of his Body. By the same token, there is a much more urgent task facing conservatives than a misguided opposition to women priests. The credibility and integrity of the Christian faith, as a coherent body of belief and practice, is not damaged, but rather enhanced, by ordaining women. But it is seriously threatened by the postmodern dissolution of culture and community. None of us wants to be found barking up the wrong tree.

Some see the ordination of women as the thin end of a liberal agenda based on feminist theology, as though that were enough to condemn it. Feminist theology does indeed expose and critique all forms of sexism, patriarchy and androcentrism in the Christian tradition, including the Bible – and there is plenty of material there for it to work on. But those who condemn feminist theology and all its works often fail to distinguish between Christian and post-Christian forms of feminist theology. There are many Christian theologians, working loyally within the community of the Church, both women and men, whose thinking has been shaped by this critique and who might, therefore, perhaps be described as feminist theologians. But there are others – the post-Christian feminist theologians such as Mary Daly (Daly, 1986) and Daphne Hampson (Hampson, 1990) – who are alienated from the Christian Church, its beliefs, worship and ministry. They believe that Christianity is so indelibly sexist that it is irredeemable. It cannot reform itself by purging out its sexism without becoming a different religion – or, more likely, self-destructing. They therefore have little interest now in the ordination of women, perhaps viewing it from afar with ironic amusement.

Though I am one of those who believes that the contribution of Christian feminist theology ought to be taken seriously (and have tried to contribute to it myself: see Avis, 1989), I do not regard the ordination of women as bound up with individual human rights, or self-expression and self-fulfilment or a sceptical relativism with regard to theological truth (all presumably items on a truly liberal agenda), but rather as arising out of a profound respect for the doctrine of holy order – as a reform and enlargement of catholic order within a renewed tradition.

Summary
There are four main objections to the ordination of women priests by the Church of England: (a) Fundamental

tradition cannot change. In reply to this argument put forward by the Vatican we agree that doctrine cannot change but claim that the outward order of the Church needs to be reformed from time to time. (b) Only the whole Church can act on a fundamental matter of holy order. We note that this is not readily compatible with (a) and in reply we insist on the authority of particular Churches to act in good faith in the absence of ecumenical instruments for decision-making at a universal level. (c) The Church of England's unilateral action is damaging to ecumenical relations. In response, we regret this, but point out that ecumenical relations are with the whole Anglican Communion, not just the Church of England. (d) Women priests are part of a liberal agenda, including militant feminism, that has designs on the whole gamut of Christian beliefs. In reply, we argue that attitudes to the issue of women's ordination have indeed been shaped as a reaction, positive or negative, to liberalism, and that too often the emancipation of women in the Church has been a nominal gesture as a way of claiming politically correct credentials, rather than a substantial, far-reaching reform. As far as feminist theology is concerned, we should distinguish between Christian and post-Christian forms and consider its critique of sexism and patriarchy in the Christian tradition, including Scripture, on its merits. Ultimately, however, the ordination of women to the priesthood is an ecclesiological matter which must be justified in terms of the fullness of Christ in all the baptised members of his Body.

Anglican Orders and the Priesting of Women

The papal bull *Apostolicae Curae* of 13 September 1896 condemned Anglican orders as 'absolutely null and utterly void'. Anglican priests were not priests and Anglican bishops were not bishops. In attacking Anglican orders, the bull undermined the means of grace provided in the Church of England and other Anglican Churches and thereby negated their claim to be regarded as true Christian Churches. Without a real ordained priesthood, Anglicans had no real sacraments and so could not provide the way of salvation. Today questions are raised, not only by the Roman Catholic Church but also within the Anglican Communion, about the validity of the orders of women priests, which are said by some Anglicans to be 'doubtful'.

Just over a century ago it was supposed doctrinal inadequacies as to eucharistic sacrifice and the nature of priesthood (defects of 'intention' and 'form') in the Anglican Ordinal which were the grounds of the Vatican's condemnation (not, as is often assumed, any supposed lack of pedigree in the succession of ordinations). The Pope argued that the Anglican Ordinal of 1662 (like those of 1550 and 1552) lacked any clear reference to the priestly power to consecrate and offer sacrifice. Moreover, he claimed that all such references had been deliberately removed. The 'native character and spirit' of the Ordinal was unmasked as blatantly uncatholic. Anglicans did not ordain with the objective intention to do what the Church does in making priests. The papal argument is vulnerable to accusations of inconsistency, illogicality and inaccuracy. The Anglican reply was not slow to exploit these. Roman Catholic scholars have tended to decline to defend the more specific claims of *Apostolicae Curae*, but have regarded its general indictment of the 'native character and spirit' of the Anglican Ordinal as the bull's strongest plank (see Clark, 1956).

At the present time, however, the point of contention is the authority claimed by the Churches of the Anglican Communion to ordain women to the priesthood. The authority of a Church to ordain is closely related to its integrity as a Christian Church. It is precisely this connection between holy order and the standing of the Church which ordains that I hope to explore now, drawing on the arguments that raged around *Apostolicae Curae* as a sort of case study. (For the text of *Apostolicae Curae* see Hill and Yarnold, eds., 1997. The background is given in Hughes, 1968, and more recent perspectives in Franklin, ed., 1996, and Franklin and Tavard, 1990.)

This papal decree, which dashed all hopes of rapprochement between the Anglican and Roman Communions for three-quarters of a century, is notorious, but the remarkable reply (*Saepius Officio*) issued by the Archbishops of Canterbury and York on the advice of the most learned bishops of the Church of England of the time is less well known. The text of the Anglican reply was drafted by John Wordsworth, Bishop of Salisbury, a consummate Latinist, who had researched the matter of Anglican orders with a view to vindicating them in ecumenical overtures to the Swedish Lutherans and the Dutch Old Catholics (who had needed to be convinced that the Church of England maintained 'the Apostolic Succession'). Wordsworth consulted with William Stubbs, Bishop of Oxford, the most erudite and prolific British medieval historian of his time, and Mandell Creighton, then Bishop of Peterborough, later of London, who was renowned for having written a multi-volume history of the papacy while he was parish priest of Embleton, and on the strength of that had been elected Dixie Professor of Ecclesiastical History at Cambridge.

The draft text of the *Responsio* reached Archbishop Edward Benson on the day before he died (as the guest of Gladstone at Hawarden). Benson was an extremely learned, astute and perceptive archbishop. Like most churchmen of his time he was a virulent critic of the papacy and held a one-sided view of the English Reformation. His longing for the reunion of Christendom took just as much account of the Eastern Churches and the non-episcopal Protestant Churches as it did of the Roman Catholic Church. Before the débâcle of 1896, Benson wrote to Lord Halifax, the indefatigable Anglo-Catholic layman who tended to take a very rosy view of Rome and of the prospects for reunion: 'If they did acknowledge our Orders, it would not alter *our* view of our position ... *their* coming to a sensible and historical standpoint ... would not settle the Roman controversy.' The Church of England would be no nearer to reunion with Rome than the Orthodox Churches were (Benson, 1900, vol. 2, pp. 611, 614). Benson was highly suspicious of Rome's motives in initiating the review of Anglican orders. If he had taken a further hand in revising the Anglican reply it would have been even more devastating than it was. He earlier privately expressed the view that the Pope's business was to eat dust and ashes (ibid., p. 586). Benson's initial response, left in draft at his death, insisted that the Church of England had a much more scholarly approach to the matter than Rome. Anglican researches had shown that 'our Holy Orders are identical with those of the whole Catholic Church. They are in origin, continuity, matter, form, intention, and all that belongs to them, identical accordingly with those of the Church of Rome, except in the one modern point of subjection to the Pope, on which point at the Reformation we deliberately resumed our ancient concurrence with the whole Catholic world besides' (ibid., p. 624).

Benson's successor as Archbishop of Canterbury, Frederick Temple (1821-1902), took it upon himself to 'cut out all the thunder'. Actually, Temple had not been unduly perturbed by the bull, being himself entirely 'convinced that the Church of England was unquestionably preferable to any other manifestation of Christianity' (Hinchcliffe, 1998, p. 265). In his ecclesiology Temple stood in the old pre-Tractarian mainstream high church tradition. He personally contributed material on the controversial areas of eucharistic sacrifice and the form of a sacrament to the response. Under Temple's supervision, the Church of England's reply to this lethal challenge to its ecclesial integrity was robust, dignified and cool, while nevertheless addressing the Pope in fraternal and charitable terms. The reply accurately pointed out that the bull was 'aimed at overthrowing our whole position as a Church'. It significantly agreed with the Pope that matter, form and intention were vital in sacramental actions, but claimed that the Anglican Ordinal met these requirements in every respect. The Archbishops stated the Anglican position on the nature of priesthood and eucharistic sacrifice in a biblical and evangelical spirit, and in accord with *The Book of Common Prayer*. This passage in particular deserves to be better known.

> We make provision with the greatest reverence for the consecration of the holy Eucharist and commit it only to properly ordained Priests and to no other ministers of the Church. Further we truly teach the doctrine of Eucharistic sacrifice and do not believe it to be a 'nude commemoration of the Sacrifice of the Cross'... But we think it sufficient in the Liturgy which we use in celebrating the holy Eucharist, - while lifting up our hearts to the Lord, and when now consecrating the gifts already offered that they may become to us the Body and Blood of our Lord Jesus Christ, - to signify the sacrifice which is offered at that point of the service in such terms as these.

The Archbishops then set out their understanding of eucharistic sacrifice. In this they tacitly distinguished between an Anglican understanding of eucharistic sacramental sacrifice and the Roman Catholic doctrine of propitiatory actual sacrifice.

> We continue a perpetual memory of the precious death of Christ, who is our Advocate with the Father and the propitiation for our sins, according to His precept, until his coming again. For first we offer the sacrifice of praise and thanksgiving; then next we plead and re-present before the Father the sacrifice of the Cross, and

> by it we confidently entreat remission of sins and all other benefits of the Lord's Passion for all the whole Church; and lastly we offer the sacrifice of ourselves to the Creator of all things which we have already signified by the oblation of His creatures.

The passage concludes: 'This whole action, in which the people has necessarily to take its part with the Priest, we are accustomed to call the Eucharistic sacrifice' (Hill and Yarnold, eds., 1997, pp. 292f.).

The Archbishops claimed that the Anglican Ordinal was actually superior to the Roman one, because it more clearly reflected Christ's intentions and the practice of the universal Church. They showed with crushing effect that the papal doctrine of what was required in holy order was an innovation, and argued *ad hominem* that 'in overthrowing our orders, he overthrows all his own, and pronounces sentence on his own Church' (Hill and Yarnold, eds., 1997, p. 316). They forthrightly defended the Reformation and the right and duty of particular Churches to reform themselves:

> He who interprets the articles of our Church by mere conjecture and takes it upon himself to issue a new decree as to what is necessary in the form of Order, condemning our lawful bishops in their government of the Church in the XVIth century by a standard which they never knew, is entering on a slippery and dangerous path. The liberty of national Churches to reform their own rites may not thus be removed at the pleasure of Rome. (Hill and Yarnold, eds., 1997, p. 305)

Thankfully, the tone of ecumenical discourse is now

very different. Courtesy, charity and genuine friendship between Anglican and Roman Catholic Church leaders has replaced the hostile, defensive and admonitory style of a century ago. The valuable work of the Anglican-Roman Catholic International Commission has created a genuine consensus on key ecclesiological issues (ARCIC, 1982). As Henry Chadwick has pointed out, ARCIC has had 'the unintended side-effect of destroying the central argument of *Apostolicae Curae*, viz. that Roman Catholics and Anglicans are committed to essentially different beliefs about the eucharistic presence and sacrifice and consequently about the nature and office of ministerial priesthood' (Chadwick, 1994, p. 92; cf. Boulding *et al.*, 1996).

Yet some of the issues that were at stake then remain unresolved. *Apostolicae Curae* has not been retracted. It still has its full force. The fact that the Roman Catholic Church has condemned the decision of the Church of England and of other Churches of the Anglican Communion to ordain women to the priesthood has highlighted the reality that Rome does not accept the orders of Anglican male priests either. The ordination of women by the Church of England, within the already given context of the unresolved argument with Rome over Anglican orders, raises two particular questions. We could call them the question of apostolicity and the question of catholicity.

- The first question, the question of apostolicity, concerns the standing of the Church of England (and by implication the standing of those other Churches of the Anglican Communion that have ordained women priests) as an authentic part, portion or branch of the one, holy, catholic and apostolic Church. The issue can be put like this: is a Church, claiming to have the threefold ministry of bishops, priests and deacons in historical succession and to share this with the Roman Catholic and Eastern Orthodox Churches, still a true and apostolic Church of Christ when it has effected a change in the apostolic ministry by ordaining women priests – a change, moreover, that those other two great communions vehemently condemn?

- The second question, the question of catholicity, concerns the security and authenticity of the holy orders of those women who have been ordained to the priesthood in the Church of England (and in other Anglican Churches). The issue can be put like this: are the holy orders of women priests, ordained in the Church of England and sister Churches of the Anglican Communion, real and authentic holy orders – ministries of the Christian Church – or are Anglican women priests merely masquerading as priests or presbyters, deceiving themselves and some of us?

Is a Church Which Ordains Women a True Church? The Question of Apostolicity

It is necessarily entailed in being a member of any Christian Church that you believe that Church to be truly a Church. If you ceased to believe that, you would go elsewhere. The authoritative formularies of the Church of England affirm, in the very first of the Canons, that

> The Church of England, established according to the laws of this realm under the Queen's Majesty, belongs to the true and apostolic Church of Christ; and, as our duty to the said Church of England requires, we do

> constitute and ordain that no member thereof shall be at liberty to maintain or hold the contrary. (Canon A1)

It may seem superfluous for a Church to insist that it is the Church and officious for the Church of England to claim to police the views of its members (which must here mean the clergy, since most of the laity are not readily subject to discipline). But it is actually vital for every Church to profess that it sees itself as an expression of the one, holy, catholic and apostolic Church of Christ.

Recent ecumenical theology is helping us to see both how fundamental the apostolicity of the Church is and how this fundamental attribute must be predicated of the whole Church. The apostolicity of the Church refers to its origin and its mission and links the two together. The Church is both grounded in the apostolic witness to Jesus Christ and perpetuates that witness. Apostolicity is concerned with the authenticity of the Church. It confronts the question of whether the Church is true to its God-given purpose. The Church is called to perpetuate the mission that Jesus Christ received from the Father and entrusted to the apostles in the dynamic of the Holy Spirit. In his High Priestly Prayer, Jesus says, 'As you have sent me into the world, so I have sent them into the world' (John 17:18). But the key text is John 20:19-21:

> Jesus came and stood among them and said, 'Peace be with you.' After he said this, he showed them his hands and his side. Then the disciples rejoiced when they saw the Lord. Jesus said to them again, 'Peace be with you. As the Father has sent me, so I send you.' When he had said this, he breathed on them and said to them, 'Receive the Holy Spirit. If you forgive the sins of any,

they are forgiven them; if you retain the sins of any, they are retained.'

Here we find several themes powerfully combined together: the risen Christ's blessing of peace upon the disciples, the abiding prints of his passion that will mark for ever the mission of the Church, the sending forth in his name in union with the Father's purpose, the authority to absolve, and the power of the Spirit that will make all this possible.

Modern biblical interpretation tends to take this 'apostling' of the first Christians to apply not just to the Twelve but to the whole Body. John simply calls them the disciples and they appear to include the women who brought the first news of the resurrection. Those gathered behind locked doors are the representative Church, the Church in embryo, the faithful remnant. Hoskyns and Davey's commentary, though half a century old, is still worth quoting:

> The controversy whether the commission is given to the Church as a whole or to the apostles is irrelevant. There is no distinction here between the Church and the ministry; both completely overlap. The evangelist records the birth of the Church as the organism of the spirit of God, and the origin of the authority of the ministry. Both are inaugurated together... The Christian community was, at its inception, a community of Apostles. (Hoskyns and Davey, pp. 545f.)

Certainly, the ecumenical theology that underlies such significant agreements as the draft Concordat between American Lutherans (Evangelical Lutheran Church of

America) and American Anglicans (The Episcopal Church of the USA), the Meissen Common Statement between the Church of England and the Evangelical (Lutheran, Reformed and United) Churches of Germany, and the Porvoo Common Statement between the British and Irish Anglican Churches and the Nordic and Baltic Lutheran Episcopal Churches recognises that the apostolicity of the Church resides in the mission of the whole Church (see *[Concordat]*, *[Meissen]* and *[Porvoo]* in bibliography).

The principle of the inalienable apostolicity of the whole people of God was stated splendidly in *Baptism, Eucharist and Ministry*, the Lima Statement of the Faith and Order Commission of the World Council of Churches, in 1982:

> In the Creed, the Church confesses itself to be apostolic. The Church lives in continuity with the apostles and their proclamation. The same Lord who sent the apostles continues to be present in the Church. The Spirit keeps the Church in the apostolic tradition until the fulfilment of history in the kingdom of God. Apostolic tradition in the Church means continuity in the permanent characteristics of the Church of the apostles: witness to the apostolic faith, proclamation and fresh interpretation of the Gospel, celebration of baptism and the eucharist, the transmission of ministerial responsibilities, communion in prayer, love, joy and suffering, service to the sick and the needy, unity among the local churches and sharing the gifts which the Lord has given to each. (BEM:34, p. 28)

The Lima Statement goes on directly to ground succession in ministry in the continuity of the whole Church.

'The primary manifestation of apostolic succession is to be found in the apostolic tradition of the Church as a whole. The succession is an expression of the permanence and, therefore, of the continuity of Christ's own mission in which the Church participates' (BEM:35, pp. 28f.). Thus succession of ordinations is one of the ways in which the apostolicity that resides in the whole body of the Church and permeates its entire life is expressed. It neither creates nor guarantees that apostolicity but is an effectual sign of it. It follows that to challenge the apostolicity of ordinations in a Church is to challenge the apostolicity of that Church. Conversely, to recognise a Church as an apostolic Church of Christ carries with it recognition of its ministry as an expression and instrument of that apostolicity.

There is a sad irony in the fact that while a number of Churches worldwide are moving to a mutual acknowledgement of their apostolicity – as mutual recognition is distinguished from structural reconciliation as a prior stage in the quest for unity – some opponents of the ordination of women have challenged the fundamental integrity of the Church of England (or of other Anglican Churches) as part of the Church of Christ. They maintain that the priesting of women is such a grievous error that it has called into question the apostolicity of their Church, making it no longer a true Church. By extrapolation, of course, they say the same of all other Churches of the Anglican Communion that have ordained women. This argument was deployed in the General Synod debate of November 1992 on the legislation to make possible the ordination of women priests. Many who hold this view have already left the Church of England. Were they right to do so?

I am reluctantly driven to the conclusion that any individuals who have reached this definite position – who believe that their Church has forfeited its apostolicity – cannot be expected to remain Anglicans. It would not be right to put moral pressure on them to stay in the teeth of this conviction. They are the ones who should feel free, in all conscience, to depart in search of a Church about whose apostolicity and authenticity as a true Church they are assured. But I would add two caveats.

First, of course, I believe they are mistaken in thinking that the Church of England has forfeited its apostolicity. Needless to say, I do not accept their premise that ordaining women has this effect. But I think they are right to set such store by the credal marks of the Church and to see that these have implications for the Church's ministry. They have drawn the wrong conclusion. One could almost say that they have done the wrong thing for the right reason.

Second, I want to insist that they are the only ones who would be justified in taking that step. Separation from and breaking communion with those with whom we are already in communion cannot be justified on lesser grounds. A study of the grounds of separation in the New Testament suggests that it is justified only when the fundamental baptismal faith is denied. Only what cuts us off from communion with Father, Son and Holy Spirit can be allowed to cut us off sacramentally from one another (see Avis, 1990, ch. 5). As Henry Chadwick has eloquently put it, 'To refuse or to withdraw from participation in the sacrament, through which the unity of the Church is effected as a concrete reality, is an exquisitely painful denial of everything we understand to be the Lord's intention for his people' (Chadwick, 1994, p. 89).

Cardinal Ratzinger underlines the point when he states: 'The unity among themselves of the communities that celebrate the eucharist is not an external accessory for eucharistic ecclesiology but its inmost condition' (Ratzinger, 1988, p. 11).

We grieve at the departure of those who deny the apostolicity of our Church and we question the logic that leads to it, but we respect the conscience that commands it. However, in order to take that step, these individuals would have to convince themselves and their Church, I suggest, on one crucial point. They would have to justify theologically the highly paradoxical position that the Church of England and large tracts of the Anglican Communion had forfeited apostolicity in the very act of practising it – by 'apostling', that is to say, commissioning or ordaining certain persons whom it judged fit candidates for that apostling. That reflection does not in itself, of course, justify the ordination of women, nor does it entail that the Church can never abuse its apostolic authority; but it does, I believe, effectively transfer the onus of proof on to those who claim that the Church's apostolicity has been misused in this way.

It would appear to be not at all an easy task to claim that a Church whose apostolic credentials had survived many vicissitudes – separation from the Roman see, unilateral changes to its doctrine and worship, abandonment of the centuries-old rule of clerical celibacy, erastianism, nepotism, time-serving clergy, unorthodox bishops, neglect of the eucharist, persecution of dissenters (including Roman Catholics), and (by their lights) ordination of women to the diaconate – then had ceased, by a single action undertaken in good faith, to be a true Church. That position divorces the ministry from the Church with a vengeance and fractures the reality of apostolicity. The paradox is intensified when we recall that the Church of England itself, at the time of the Reformation, refused to condemn the Church of Rome as no true Church for all its appalling faults, errors and corruptions. I must confess that I do not see how such individuals could satisfy themselves and their Church on that point.

How Secure Are the Orders of Women Priests? The Question of Catholicity

One objection to the ordination of women by Anglican Churches that, as I have said, I take entirely seriously is that a part of the Church lacks the authority to make a change in the ministry which belongs to the whole Church. Issues concerning parts and wholes of the Church are issues of catholicity. Catholicity I take to have to do with the universality and therefore the completeness or fullness of the Church. A unilateral decision in an area where the Church should act in an undivided way damages the catholicity of the Church. This is a difficulty that perhaps exercises particularly those who remain Anglicans – who do not believe that the ordination of women priests was an act of self-destruction on the part of Anglican Churches – but who cannot accept the orders of those women priests and who therefore feel compelled to boycott their priestly ministry of word and sacrament. There is a paradox in this position also: it suggests that one can accept the apostolic authority of a given Church but reject the way in which it has canonically exercised that apostolicity.

The Canons of the Church of England intensify the difficulty for those with scruples about the priesting of women when they assert that those who are 'made, ordained, or consecrated bishops, priests, or deacons, according to the said Ordinal, are lawfully made, ordained, or consecrated, and ought to be accounted, both by themselves and others, to be truly bishops, priests, or deacons' (Canon A4).

However, the Church of England's Episcopal Ministry Act of Synod 1993 gave conscientious objectors to women priests the right to decline to accept the holy orders of women lawfully priested under the Ordinal. The legislation of 1992 had already written into it the possibility of parishes declining the ministry of women priests and it allowed for the possibility of 'no-go' dioceses on the decision of the bishop. Thus the Act of Synod itself is not to blame for the situation where the priesthood of women may be lawfully declined. However, the Act of Synod did seem to go further in acknowledging opposition to women's priesthood as an equally legitimate position within the Church of England. The phrase in vogue in some quarters is that the orders of women priests are of 'doubtful validity'.

It might be argued that the Act of Synod qualifies the full force of the Canon, though others might question whether an Act of Synod has sufficient constitutional authority to do this. In practice, however, it certainly does blunt the bold affirmation of the Canons as to the genuineness of Anglican orders. One might well question whether, in the light of *Apostolicae Curae*, the Church of England has been wise to introduce any note of uncertainty into its historic defence of its orders. In allowing the genuineness (I am trying to avoid the vexed term 'validity' as much as possible) of the priestly ordination of women to be questioned, are we not giving hostages to fortune by implying that it is at least sometimes permissible to question Anglican orders? Few will deny, I think, that there is a serious ambiguity here.

Be that as it may, a person who remained uneasy about women priests but did not regard this step as so heinous as to negate the apostolicity of the Church of England and render it no true Church, so causing them to depart elsewhere, might care to consider the following argument. If the Church of England does indeed remain an apostolic Church, then it certainly has the authority to ordain whomsoever it deems fit subjects for holy orders. The orders that it bestows on its female ordinands are the same orders that it bestows on its male ordinands. Women priests have exactly the same assurance as their male colleagues that in their case the Church is doing what it has the authority to do. There is no difference. Canon A4, which insists that those who are ordained according to the Ordinal are lawfully ordained 'and ought to be accounted both by themselves and others to be truly bishops, priests, or deacons' has equal relevance to men and women clergy. Ordination is God's action, performed through the Church. It is God who makes priests (or other ministers) by the power of the Holy Spirit, not the Church's liturgy. Though ministers are not self-appointing – as the 1662 Ordinal insists, no one can be accounted a deacon, priest or bishop in the Church of England unless they have received episcopal ordination – yet there is a sense in which the Church is merely acknowledging the prevenient act of the Holy Spirit in calling a person to a particular ministry and bestowing the necessary gifts on them (see Bradshaw in Holeton, ed., 1997). Those who ordain intend to do what the Church does. The Council of Florence declared in 1439: 'All the sacraments are effected by three elements, namely by material things as the matter, by words as the form, and by the person of the minister conferring the sacrament with the intention of doing what the Church does.' Where that has indeed been the intention, performed in good faith, it is not easy to see how the result can be gainsaid. That is the line Anglicans take against Rome over the ordination of male priests. The same logic seems to suggest that the ordination of women priests should be taken with equal seriousness. What the Church does in fact is to recognise the mysterious work of the Holy Spirit and follow the Spirit's sovereign lead.

However, some opponents of women priests take the line that, while the orders of Anglican male clergy are securely catholic and apostolic because they are recognised by parts of the Church beyond the Anglican Communion, the orders of women clergy are of 'doubtful validity' because they are not so recognised. Let us look more closely at this tactic.

The Churches that recognise the validity of the orders of Anglican (male) clergy are – apart from the Reformation and post-Reformation Protestant Churches which are not considered relevant at this point by the proponents of the argument we are considering – the Old Catholics and some Orthodox Churches, including the Patriarchate of Constantinople. Since most provinces of the Old Catholic Church are now moving towards ordaining women and the implications of this are uncertain, let us confine ourselves to the Orthodox (see Limouris, ed., 1994, Hardy, ed., 1946, and Fouyas, 1972, pp. 99-106).

Orthodox recognition, where it has been forthcoming, seems to be confined to the conditional acceptance of

Anglican orders and is given in reply to the question, if an Anglican priest converts to Orthodoxy, should he be (re)ordained? That question points to the hypothetical character of Orthodox recognition of Anglican orders, though even as such it is certainly to be welcomed and esteemed. But the Orthodox do not recognise any Christian Church other than their own. It is incompatible with Orthodox ecclesiology to acknowledge any other Church as catholic and apostolic. The Orthodox are not in communion with us and do not recognise any degrees of 'intercommunion' short of unity in faith and unity in the bishop, that is to say, unity in Orthodoxy. Some do not even recognise Anglican baptisms, let alone orders. The Orthodox Church has repeatedly declined to make a public judgement on the question of recognition of non-Orthodox baptisms, even Roman Catholic baptisms (Greek Orthodox sometimes rebaptise Roman Catholics). Thus it has not reciprocated the Second Vatican Council's recognition of the validity of Orthodox sacraments in its Decree on Ecumenism (Lanne, 1985, p. 26).

How meaningful is it to claim that some Orthodox Churches recognise Anglican orders when they do not even recognise the Church of England as a Church within which those orders are exercised? It seems a rather tenuous argument that defends Anglican (male) orders on the basis of Orthodox support. We ought surely to face the fact that it is the Church of England alone, though as part of the Anglican Communion, that bestows ordination upon its clergy, male and female alike. Their only real security is given entirely within the Anglican context.

Sometimes the decision to admit women to the priesthood is criticised on the grounds that it makes Roman

Catholic acceptance of Anglican orders impossible. It is sometimes alleged that the Anglican-Roman Catholic International Commission (ARCIC) was on the verge of an agreement on Anglican orders when the Church of England decided to ordain women priests. This gambit is supported by the exchange of letters between Archbishop Robert Runcie and Pope John Paul II in 1988, when the Pope warned that this would create a grave obstacle to closer relations between the two communions. If it is really the case that ARCIC was in sight of a breakthrough on this issue, that is one more feather in its cap and confirms the importance and success of this dialogue. But it is still a very far cry indeed from official Roman Catholic acceptance of Anglican orders. Rome's response to the *Final Report* (1982) and the Sacred Congregation for the Doctrine of the Faith's comments on the report on justification *Salvation and the Church* show all too clearly that the Roman Catholic representatives on ARCIC cannot speak for the Vatican.

However, let us suppose that further ecumenical convergence removed the theological objections alleged by *Apostolicae Curae*: that would not in itself bring recognition of Anglican orders, that is to say, of the ministries of priests and bishops in the Church of England and the Churches of the Anglican Communion. It is because Anglicans are not within the Roman obedience and therefore not in communion with the Pope, through whom all hierarchical and sacramental power is held to flow, that, like other separated Churches, it is regarded as deficient in the grace of orders and therefore in the power to celebrate the eucharist. Vatican II's decree on ecumenism (*Unitatis Redintegratio [UR]*) recognises that baptism 'constitutes a sacramental bond of unity' between all the baptised. But baptism in itself, it claims, is not sufficient. It is, says the decree, 'only a beginning, a point of departure, for it is wholly directed toward the acquiring of fullness of life in Christ.' It is orientated towards 'a complete incorporation into the system of salvation' intended by Christ (UR:22; Abbott, ed., 1966, p. 364). It is because separated Churches (Vatican II does not call them Churches, but 'ecclesial bodies') are not incorporated into that 'system' that they lack sacramental fullness. The decree on the Church (*Lumen Gentium [LG]*) corroborates this when it says:

> They are fully incorporated into the society of the Church who, possessing the Spirit of Christ, accept her entire system and all the means of salvation given to her, and through union with her visible structure are joined to Christ, who rules her through the Supreme Pontiff and the bishops. This joining is effected by the bonds of professed faith, of the sacraments, of ecclesiastical government, and of communion. (LG:14; Abbott, ed., 1966, p. 3)

The emphasis is on rule, government, obedience and unity of structure.

That is the background to the Vatican Council's rejection of the orders of separated communities (other than the Orthodox of course, who constitute a special case). The decree on ecumenism pronounces:

> The ecclesial communities separated from us lack that fullness of unity with us which should flow from baptism, and we believe that especially because of the lack of the sacrament of orders they have not preserved the

genuine and total reality of the Eucharistic mystery. (UR:22; Abbott, ed., 1966, p. 364)

It is not just a question of technical validity or even of agreement on the doctrines of the priesthood and eucharistic sacrifice. It is ultimately a question of obedience to the claims of the papacy – as was repeatedly pointed out by Mandell Creighton at the time of *Apostolicae Curae* (see Creighton, 1904, vol. 2, pp. 177-83). In my opinion, it is highly unlikely that Rome would give a form of recognition to Anglican ministries and sacraments that would give succour to the notion of the Anglican Communion as 'an alternative and rival Catholicism' (Chadwick, 1994, p. 91). The Vatican does not recognise the distinction that is proving so useful in much ecumenical work, between acknowledgement of one another as true Churches with authentic ministries and sacraments, on the one hand, and integration with one another in some degree of visible unity that would entail, for example, interchangeability of ministries, on the other. Both Rome and the Orthodox find this distinction invidious. The report of the 1987 meeting at Bari of the Joint International Commission for Theological Dialogue between the Roman Catholic Church and the Orthodox Church significantly stated: 'Communion is possible only between those Churches which have faith, priesthood and the sacraments in common' (21). 'Communion in faith and communion in the sacraments,' it affirmed, 'are not two distinct realities. They are two aspects of a single reality' (36) (see *Faith, Sacraments and the Unity of the Church*). For both Rome and Orthodoxy, unity in faith is not something that can be agreed as a restricted agenda separate from acceptance of the distinctive claims of those Churches. Faith is precisely 'the obedience of faith'.

So it is, frankly, wishful thinking to imagine that the question of Anglican orders could be settled in isolation from the question of Anglican acceptance of the claims of the papacy, including the definitive, binding authority of the magisterium and the universal immediate jurisdiction of the papacy. It seems that the genuineness or 'validity' (if we must use that word) of Anglican orders will have to be decided for a long time to come on the basis of Anglican, rather than Roman claims.

What then is the status of the orders of Anglican women priests? As will be clear by now, I find the suggestion that the orders of women priests are of 'doubtful validity' because they are not accepted by the largest and most ancient Christian Churches, while the orders of male priests are valid in spite of not being accepted by those Churches, far too paradoxical for my taste. If the Church of England and the other Churches of the Anglican Communion, being parts or portions of the catholic and apostolic Church of Christ, have in the exercise of that catholic and apostolic authority, admitted women to holy orders, then it is to be hoped that all of us will in due course be able to accept them. It remains a defensible position to hold that these Anglican Churches have 'jumped the gun' ecumenically, but this cannot undo what the Church has done. What the Church of England has done in the case of women priests is identical with what it has done in the case of male priests. Those who go so far as to deny the reality of the orders of women priests actually undermine their own.

Summary

As we continue to evaluate the Church of England's decision to ordain women to the priesthood in the light of the nature of the Church, two questions arise. They both concern Anglican orders which are not recognised by the Roman Catholic Church. First, one might ask whether a Church that makes a change in the received structure of holy order, which is acknowledged as an aspect of the Church's essential apostolicity, thereby damages its apostolicity. How can we know whether such a Church is a true Christian Church? The answer offered is that apostolicity should be understood in the light of recent ecumenical theology where it is postulated of the whole ongoing life of the Church, lived in intended continuity with the apostles. The commissioning or 'apostling' of ministers is one expression of this broad apostolicity. Second, one might ask whether the ordination to the priesthood that such women have received is certain or in fact doubtful. How do we know whether their orders are secure? The answer proposed involves eliminating the tactic of adducing support from other Churches that have the threefold ministry in historical succession, as building on sand, and taking entirely seriously the claims of Anglican ecclesiology. The assurance that they give with respect to the orders of Anglican male priests, they give equally with respect to Anglican women priests.

Questions

Introduction
1. Why is it important to offer a theological justification of the ordination of women priests by the Church of England?
2. Are you aware of resources for theological reflection on this question? If so, which have you found helpful and why?
3. What is meant by a period of reception?
4. Is it appropriate to expect complete certainty on theological issues?
5. What are the main theological objections to women priests?

Objections to Women Priests
1. How has the Roman Catholic Church appealed to the authority of tradition on this point?
2. How do Anglicans tend to evaluate tradition?
3. Is the ordination of women properly seen as a doctrinal matter or a reform of practice in the sphere of order?
4. What does the expression 'the whole Church' mean in practice in a divided Christendom? Is 'unilateral action' always wrong? What responsibilities for ordering their life does the Anglican tradition give to particular Churches?
5. What weight would you give to the 'ecumenical damage' argument?
6. How have positions for or against the ordination of

women been related to liberal cultural positions?
7. What is the relevance of feminist theology to this issue?

Anglican Orders and the Priesting of Women

1. In what circumstances and on what grounds did the Roman Catholic Church condemn Anglican orders?
2. What formal response did the Church of England make?
3. How does recent ecumenical theology understand the apostolicity of the Church?
4. On what grounds is it theologically justifiable to break communion?
5. How is the question of Anglican orders related to the catholicity of the Church?
6. What view do the Eastern Orthodox Churches take of Anglican orders – and of the Anglican Churches as such?
7. What part would Roman Catholic recognition of Anglican orders play in the reconciling of the two communions?
8. How does the Church of England maintain the validity of the orders of its male clergy? Is there any difference between male and female ordinations on this score?

Bibliography

Abbott, W.M. (ed.), *The Documents of Vatican II* (London & Dublin: Geoffrey Chapman, 1966).

Anglican Orders (English): The Bull of His Holiness Leo XIII, September 13, 1896, and the Answer of the Archbishops of England, March 29, 1897 (London: SPCK, 1957).

Apostolicity and Succession, House of Bishops Occasional Paper (London: General Synod of the Church of England, 1994).

ARCIC, *The Final Report of the Anglican-Roman Catholic International Commission* (London: SPCK/CTS, 1982).

Avis, P., *Anglicanism and the Christian Church: Theological Resources in Historical Perspective* (Edinburgh: T & T Clark; Philadelphia: Fortress, 1989).

Eros and the Sacred (London: SPCK, 1989).

Christians in Communion (London: Geoffrey Chapman/Mowbray; Collegeville: Liturgical Press, 1990).

Baptism, Eucharist and Ministry, The Lima Statement (Geneva: WCC, 1982).

Benson, A.C., *The Life of Edward White Benson* (London: Macmillan, 1900).

Boulding, C., Greenacre, R., Muddiman, J., Yarnold, E., 'Apostolicae Curae: A Hundred Years On', *One in Christ* 32 (1996), pp. 295-309.

Chadwick, H., *Tradition and Exploration* (Norwich: The Canterbury Press, 1994).

Chapman, M., *By What Authority? Authority, Ministry and the Catholic Church*, Affirming Catholicism series (London: DLT, 1997).

Chaves, M., *Ordaining Women: Culture and Conflict in Religious Organizations* (Cambridge MA: Harvard

University Press, 1997).

Clark, F., *Anglican Orders and Defect of Intention* (London: Longmans, 1956).

[Concordat]. *Toward Full Communion and Concordat of Agreement*, ed. W.A. Norgren and W.G. Rusch (Minneapolis, Augsburg/Cincinnati: Forward Movement, 1991).

Creighton, L., *Life and Letters of Mandell Creighton* (London: Longmans, Green and Co., 1904), 2 vols.

Daly, M., *Beyond God the Father* (London: The Women's Press, 1986).

Eames, R., *Report of the Archbishop of Canterbury's Commission on Communion and Women in the Episcopate* (London: Church House Publishing, 1989).

Edwards, R., *The Case for Women's Ministry* (London: SPCK, 1989).

Episcopal Ministry: The Report of the Archbishops' Group on the Episcopate 1990 (London: Church House Publishing, 1990).

'Faith, Sacraments and the Unity of the Church', The Bari Statement of the RC–Orthodox International Commission, *One in Christ* 23 (1987:4), pp. 330-40.

Flannery, A. (ed.), *Vatican Council II: More Post-Conciliar Documents* (New York: Costello Publishing, 1982).

Fouyas, M., *Orthodoxy, Roman Catholicism and Anglicanism* (London: OUP, 1972).

Franklin, R.W. and Tavard, G.H., 'Commentary on ARC/USA Statement on Anglican Orders', *Journal of Ecumenical Studies*, 27:2 (1990), pp. 261-87.

Hampson, D., *Theology and Feminism* (Oxford: Blackwell, 1990).

Hardy, E.R. (ed.), *Orthodox Statements on Anglican Orders* (New York, 1946).

Hayter, M., *The New Eve in Christ* (London: SPCK, 1987).

Hill, C. and Yarnold, E. (eds.), *Anglican Orders: The Documents in the Debate* (Norwich: Canterbury Press, 1997).

Hinchcliffe, P., *Frederick Temple: Archbishop of Canterbury* (Oxford: Clarendon Press, 1998).

Holeton, D. (ed.), *Anglican Orders and Ordinations* (Cambridge: Grove Books, 1997).

Hooker, R., *Works*, ed. J. Keble (Oxford: OUP, 1845), 3 vols.

Hoskyns, E. and Davey, N., *The Fourth Gospel* (London: Faber and Faber, 1947).

Hughes, J.J., *Absolutely Null and Utterly Void* (Washington, DC and Cleveland: Corpus, 1968).

Küng, H., *Infallible?* (London: Fontana, 1972).

Lanne, E., 'Catholic-Orthodox Dialogue: in Search of a New Direction', *One in Christ* 21 (1985:1), pp. 19-30.

Limouris, G., *Orthodox Visions of Ecumenism* (Geneva: WCC, 1994).

McAdoo, H., *Anglicans and Tradition and the Ordination of Women* (Norwich: Canterbury Press, 1997).

[Meissen]. *The Meissen Agreement: Texts* (London: Council for Christian Unity, 1992).

Osborne, K.B., *Priesthood: A History of the Ordained Ministry in the Roman Catholic Church* (New Jersey: Paulist Press, 1988).

[Porvoo]. *Together in Mission and Ministry: The Porvoo Common Statement with Essays on Church and Ministry in Northern Europe* (London: Church House Publishing, 1993).

Ratzinger, J., *Church, Ecumenism and Politics* (Slough: St Paul, 1988).

Sedgwick, J., *Why Women Priests? The Ordination of Women and the Apostolic Ministry* (London: Affirming Catholicism, 1992).